The Primary Source Library of Famous Composers™

Franz Peter
Schubert

Eric Michael Summerer

The Rosen Publishing Group's
PowerKids Press™
PRIMARY SOURCE

New York

To Stefanie

Published in 2006 by The Rosen Publishing Group, Inc.
29 East 21st Street, New York, NY 10010

Copyright © 2006 by The Rosen Publishing Group, Inc.

First Edition

Editor: Frances E. Ruffin
Book Design: Michael J. Caroleo
Photo Researcher: Rebecca Anguin-Cohen

Eric "Michaels" Summerer is music director and "morning guy" at the Internet radio station Beethoven.com

Photo Credits: Cover (Schubert), pp. 7 (full page), 16 (full page) Historisches Museum der Stadt, Vienna, Austria/Bridgeman Art Library; cover and interior borders (sheet music) Library of Congress, Music Division; p. 4 Magyar Nemzeti Galeria, Budapest, Hungary/Bridgeman Art Library; pp. 7 (inset), 8, 15, 16 (inset), 19 (inset), 20 (inset), 22–23, 27 (full page) © Erich Lessing/Art Resource, NY; p. 11, Private Collection/Bridgeman Art Library; p. 12 (full page) Bibliotheque du Conservatoire de Musique, Paris, France/Bridgeman Art Library; p. 12 (inset) Kunsthistorisches Museum, Vienna, Austria/Bridgeman Art Library; p. 19 (full page) © Sandro Vannini/Corbis; p. 20 (full page) © Archivo Iconografico, SA/Corbis; p. 24 (full page) Schubert Museum, Vienna, Austria/Bridgeman Art Library; p. 24 (inset) © Scala/Art Resource, NY; p. 27 (inset) Hulton Archive/Getty Images.

Library of Congress Cataloging-in-Publication Data

Summerer, Eric Michael.
Franz Peter Schubert / Eric Michael Summerer—1st ed.
    v.cm.—(The primary source library of famous composers)
Includes bibliographical references and index.
Contents: The not so famous Schubert—The family quartet—Schubert's many instruments—Off to school—Young Schubert the teacher—Unlucky in love—Schubertiads—The trout—Little Mushroom—Serious illness—A sudden end—Unfinished symphony—Listening to Schubert.
ISBN 1-4042-2768-7 (library binding)
1. Schubert, Franz, 1797–1828—Juvenile literature. 2. Composers—Austria—Biography—Juvenile literature. [1. Schubert, Franz, 1797–1828. 2. Composers.] I. Title. II. Series.

ML3930.S38S86 2005
780'.92—dc22

2003024459

Manufactured in the United States of America

Contents

The Not-so-Famous Schubert

When Franz Peter Schubert was alive, few people had ever heard of him. Schubert was a **composer** who lived in Austria in the early nineteenth century. He was never hired to write music or to play in an **orchestra**, as many other composers were. During his life he made very little money from the music he wrote. He never even heard one of his **symphonies performed** by an orchestra. However, he loved playing music and writing new pieces for his friends, who were artists and other **musicians**. Schubert had a short life, living only 31 years, but he wrote more music than most composers write in a lifetime. When Schubert was alive, he was not famous outside his hometown, but after his death people all over the world came to love his music.

After Franz Schubert's death, a friend said of him, "He was only a little man, but he was giant."

The Family Quartet

Franz Peter Schubert was born in a small town near Vienna, Austria, on January 31, 1797. His parents were Franz and Elizabeth. He was the twelfth child in a family of 14 children. Only Franz, three brothers, and one sister lived to be adults. Schubert's father ran an elementary school from the family home. His father loved listening to music, and he played the **cello**. He taught Schubert's brothers Ignaz and Ferdinand to play the **violin**, and he taught young Franz to play the **viola**. Together, father and sons formed a **string quartet**. They played music together for fun. Schubert wrote his first musical **compositions** for his family to play.

In total, Schubert wrote more than 1,000 musical pieces. He wrote compositions for about 18 years of his life, which means that he wrote more than one piece of music every single week.

This painting shows Franz and his family playing games. Inset: Schubert's father loved playing music with his children.

When Franz Schubert was nine years old, he studied music with Michael Holzer. Holzer was the **organist** at a local church. He taught Franz how to play the **organ**, the **piano**, and the violin. He also taught Schubert how to sing.

In 1808, when Schubert was 11, a local newspaper held a **competition**. The winner would be invited to join the **choir** at the **Imperial** and Royal Chapel in Vienna. Not only was it a big honor to sing with such a famous choir, but also all the choirboys got a free education at the Imperial and Royal **Seminary**. To join the choir, Schubert had to perform in front of Antonio Salieri, the composer and musician who was in charge of the choir. Schubert was nervous, but he sang well, and Salieri chose him for the choir.

This painting shows Stadtkonvikt. Stadtkonvikt was the Imperial and Royal Seminary in Vienna, where Schubert attended school and became a choirboy.

Off to School

Schubert was in the choir with about 130 other boys, most of whom were the sons of army officers. The boys studied reading, math, and music, and they sang during the church services in the chapel. Schubert liked the uniform that he had to wear in church. He wore a dark brown coat with polished buttons, a white **neckerchief**, **knickers**, **buckled** shoes, and a three-cornered hat. Schubert studied musical composition with Salieri, and he practiced playing his violin by joining the school's orchestra. The conductor of the orchestra recognized Schubert's talent as a musician, so he made Schubert the leader of the violin section. The orchestra usually played music by other composers, but Schubert started writing his own music for the school orchestra to play.

Schubert wrote his first symphony for the school orchestra when he was 16. His musical heroes were Franz Joseph Haydn, Wolfgang Amadeus Mozart, and Ludwig van Beethoven.

Before moving to Vienna, Schubert loved to walk to school with his father. His father was Schubert's first music teacher.

Young Schubert the Teacher

When Schubert turned 15, his voice became too deep to sing with the choir. The boys who sang in the choir had to have higher voices. However, the school liked the music that Schubert wrote. They tried to give him a **scholarship** so that he could stay in school. To keep the scholarship, Schubert needed to pass all his school subjects, but he failed math. At the end of 1813, he was asked to leave school.

Schubert returned home to help teach at his father's school. The job was not hard to do, and it gave Schubert a lot of time to work on his music. His favorite kind of music to write was called lieder, which is the German word for "songs." Schubert took German and Austrian poems and set them to music. Schubert's lieder poems were to be performed by a **soloist** who sang the words and by a pianist who played the music.

Schubert wrote this lieder in 1819. Inset: Schubert is shown here in his late teens. During that time, he taught music to young children for little money.

Unlucky in Love

In 1814, Schubert wrote his first **Mass**, which is a composition that is performed in a church. Schubert's Mass was performed once at Schubert's local church and a second time at Augustine Church, in the center of Vienna. Therese Grob, a young woman soloist, sang at both performances. She was one year younger than Schubert, and she had a lovely voice. Schubert fell in love with her. He wrote many songs about his feelings for Therese. Schubert wanted to marry Therese, but his teaching job did not pay very well, and he made no money from his music. He could not prove to Therese's father that he would be able to take care of her. Their **romance** ended. In 1816, Schubert decided he did not want to teach anymore. At age 20, he left his father's home and moved in with a friend. He wanted to **concentrate** on writing music.

Schubert was in love with Therese Grob, who is shown in this painting. Inset: *Schubert played his Mass in F, shown here, on this organ in Vienna.*

Schubertiads

Schubert moved in with a law student named Franz von Schober. Schober **introduced** Schubert to many of Vienna's local artists, poets, and musicians. Soon Schubert made many new friends. Every day Schubert spent the morning writing new music, and he spent the afternoon talking with friends about **politics** or art. At night, Schubert and his friends gathered at someone's house for a party. They read poetry, played games, put on plays, and performed music. Schubert's music became so popular at these parties that people started calling the parties and the people who attended them "Schubertiads." Composing music for his friends was fun, but it did not pay Schubert's bills. In 1818, he took a summer job teaching music to the daughters of a Hungarian nobleman named Johann Esterházy.

The Schubertiads were painted by Julius Schmid. Inset: Franz von Schober introduced Schubert to Vienna's young partygoers.

"The Trout"

During the summer of 1819, Schubert went on vacation with one of his friends to Steyr. This was a little town about 90 miles (145 km) from Vienna. When Schubert was not spending time with friends, he composed music.

A few years earlier, Schubert had written the song "Die Forelle," which means "The Trout." While in Steyr, he took his song and turned it into a composition that become known as the Trout **Quintet**. A quintet is a piece of music that is played by five instruments. For the Trout Quintet, the instruments are piano, violin, viola, cello, and **double bass**. The Trout Quintet was a **variation** of the song. By using different instruments and by playing the theme faster or slower, or louder or softer, the variation turned the music into a whole new composition.

In Steyr, Austria, shown here, Schubert wrote The Trout Quintet. "The Trout" describes how a fisher tricks a fish into his net. Inset: Schubert enjoyed spending time with his friends, as seen on this ride in the countryside.

Schubert was a short man, little more than 5 feet (1.5 m) tall. He had curly black hair, and he wore wire-rimmed glasses. As he got older, he started to get fat as well. His friends called him Schwammerl, which means "Tubby," or "Little Mushroom." In Austria, men between ages 18 and 45 were required to spend at least 14 years in the army. Only men who had certain jobs, such as doctors or students, could avoid this period in the army. Musicians were also considered important and could avoid the army. To get out of fighting, Schubert had to prove that he was paid to write music. However, he lived mostly off of the kindness of his friends. Fortunately, Schubert was too short and his eyesight was too bad for him to serve in the army.

Schubert was able to avoid serving in the Austrian army during the Napoleonic Wars, which were fought from 1799 to 1815. Here the French are shown in a battle with the Austrians during one of the wars. Inset: Schubert was called Little Mushroom by his friends.

At the end of 1822, Schubert felt very unwell. Around his twenty-sixth birthday, he learned that he had a serious **disease**. At that time, there was no cure for the illness. The best **treatment** was injecting the person with **mercury**. Mercury is a liquid metal that is also a poison. Using mercury as medicine was very painful and **dangerous**. Schubert stayed in

Schubert offered his Ninth Symphony, "Great C-major," to the Society of Music Lovers in Vienna. They turned it down, saying that the piece was too hard for their musicians to play.

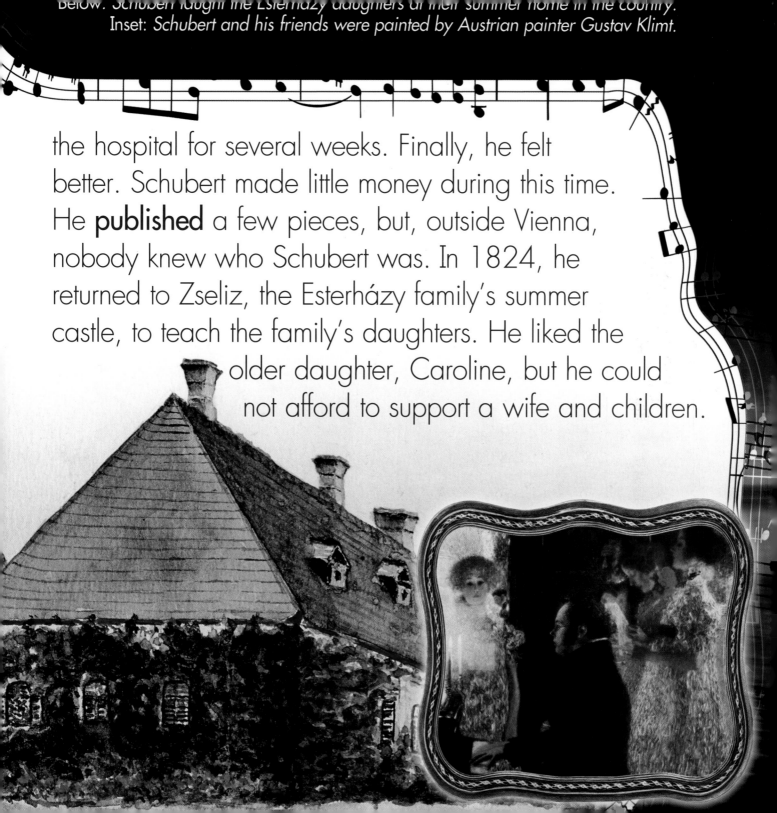

the hospital for several weeks. Finally, he felt better. Schubert made little money during this time. He **published** a few pieces, but, outside Vienna, nobody knew who Schubert was. In 1824, he returned to Zseliz, the Esterházy family's summer castle, to teach the family's daughters. He liked the older daughter, Caroline, but he could not afford to support a wife and children.

Schubert held his first and only full-scale public **concert** in March 1828. It was called Schubert's Invitation Concert. Schubert played the piano with a choir and a string quartet. His **audience** loved the concert, but the newspapers did not **review** it. Most of the people in Vienna were too busy listening to a concert by a famous violinist named Niccolò Paganini, who had a sold-out concert that same night. As the year went on, Schubert's illness worsened. By fall, his doctor told Schubert to move in with his brother Ferdinand and to stay in bed. On November 19, 1828, Schubert turned to his brother, said, "Here, here is my end," and died. He was only 31 years old. Schubert was buried in a Vienna **cemetery** near the composer Ludwig van Beethoven.

This piano belonged to Schubert. Inset: *Violinist Niccolò Paganini is shown performing in concert. Schubert's concert was not well attended because people were listening to Paganini play.*

In his last years, Schubert read many books. American author James Fenimore Cooper's book *The Last of the Mohicans* was one of Schubert's favorites.

"Unfinished Symphony"

After Schubert's death, many compositions were found in his home that had not been performed. One was a symphony that would later become his most famous piece. It was called Symphony No. 8. Schubert started this symphony in 1822, around the time that he became sick. Usually a symphony has four movements, or parts. The first movement is often fast, and the second is slower. The last two movements are usually quick and strong and make an exciting ending. Schubert finished only two movements of this symphony. One was fast and one was slow. Since the symphony was not complete, it became known as the "Unfinished Symphony." Nobody knows why Schubert did not finish the symphony. Some people think that working on it reminded Schubert of his illness. Others believe that Schubert just ran out of time.

Schubert's glasses lie on the sheet music for the last lieder he wrote before his death. Inset: Wearing his glasses, Schubert works on a composition.

Today Schubert is known as the master of combining words and music. Musicians who write songs today agree that they have learned about music from his compositions. Schubert's music is heard and played everywhere. His church composition "Ave Maria" is one of the most popular wedding songs. A stage play called *Death and the Maiden* is named for one of Schubert's string quartets. Countless films, from *Fantasia* to *The Sixth Sense*, use Schubert's music.

Fans of Schubert's music hold festivals, or parties, in his honor every year. The festivals are called Schubertiads, named for the parties that Schubert enjoyed with his friends. Just as Schubert's friends once gathered to hear his music, today music lovers around the world come together to do the same thing.

Listening to Schubert

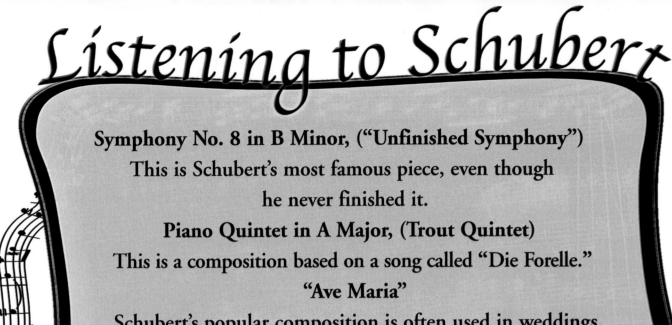

Symphony No. 8 in B Minor, ("Unfinished Symphony")
This is Schubert's most famous piece, even though
he never finished it.
Piano Quintet in A Major, (Trout Quintet)
This is a composition based on a song called "Die Forelle."
"Ave Maria"
Schubert's popular composition is often used in weddings.
"Erlkonig"
This famous song was one of Schubert's first compositions.

Timeline

1797 Franz Peter Schubert is born on January 31 near Vienna, Austria.
1806 Schubert studies music with Michael Holzer.
1808 Schubert attends school at Vienna's Imperial and Royal Seminary.
1815 Schubert meets Franz von Schober.
1818 Schubert publishes "Lake Erlaf."
1821 Schubert's "Erlkonig" becomes popular.
1822 Schubert begins to compose Symphony No. 8.
1823 Schubert comes down with a serious illness.
1825 Schubert composes "Ave Maria."
1828 Franz Peter Schubert dies on November 19 in Vienna.

Musical Terms

cello (CHEH-loh) A stringed instrument that creates a lower sound than a viola or a violin.

choir (KWYR) A group of people who sing together.

composer (kom-POH-zer) A person who writes music.

compositions (kom-puh-ZIH-shunz) Pieces of writing or music.

concert (KON-sert) A public musical performance.

double bass (DUH-bul BAYS) A large, low-pitched stringed instrument.

Mass (MAS) A musical piece based on a church service.

musicians (myoo-ZIH-shunz) People who write, play, or sing music.

orchestra (OR-kes-truh) A group of people who play music together.

organ (OR-gen) A keyboard instrument that makes music by driving air through pipes of different sizes.

organist (OR-geh-nist) A person who plays the organ.

performed (per-FORMD) Sang, danced, acted, or played an instrument in front of other people.

piano (pee-A-noh) An instrument with small hammers that strike wire strings to make music when its set of keys is pressed.

quintet (kwin-TET) A piece of music that is written for five instruments.

soloist (SOH-luh-wist) One who sings or plays music on his or her own.

string quartet (STRING kwor-TET) A musical group made up of four musicians who use instruments with strings, which are played with a bow or plucked.

symphonies (SIM-fuh-neez) Long musical compositions written for an orchestra.

variation (ver-ee-AY-shun) A composition that rewrites the theme of another composition but that keeps the original theme.

viola (vee-OH-luh) A stringed instrument that is lower in sound than a violin but higher than a cello.

violin (vy-uh-LIN) A small instrument that makes music by having a bow drawn over its strings.

Glossary

audience (AH-dee-ints) A group of people who watch or listen to something.

buckled (BUH-kuld) To have fastened a belt or strap with a buckle, which is a metal clasp.

cemetery (SEH-muh-ter-ee) A place where the dead are buried.

competition (kom-pih-TIH-shin) A game or test.

concentrate (KON-sen-trayt) To focus one's thoughts and attention on one thing.

dangerous (DAYN-jer-us) Able to cause harm.

disease (duh-ZEEZ) An illness or sickness.

imperial (im-PEER-ee-ul) Having to do with an empire or an emperor.

introduced (in-truh-DOOSD) To have brought into use, knowledge, or notice.

knickers (NIH-kerz) Short pants gathered at the knee.

mercury (MER-kyuh-ree) A poisonous, silver-colored element.

neckerchief (NEH-ker-chif) A scarf or cloth that is worn around the neck.

politics (PAH-lih-tiks) The science of governments and elections.

published (PUH-blishd) To have printed something so people can read it.

review (rih-VYOO) A written opinion that lists something's good and bad points.

romance (roh-MANS) A love affair.

scholarship (SKAH-ler-ship) Money given to someone to pay for school.

seminary (SEH-mih-ner-ee) A school or college for the study of religion.

treatment (TREET-ment) The act or manner of handling someone.

Index

Primary Sources

Cover. Oil on canvas portrait of Franz Peter Schubert by Willibrod Maehler (1796–1880). Schubert Museum, Vienna, Austria.

Page 4. Portrait of Schubert by Melegh Gabor (1801–1835). Magyar Nemzeti Galeria, Budapest, Hungary.

Page 7. The family of Franz Peter Schubert playing games. Leopold Kupelwieser (1796–1862). Historisches Museum der Stadt Wien, Vienna, Austria.

Page 7. Inset. Schubert's father, Franz Theodore. Carl Schubert (1795–1855). Oil on canvas. Historisches Museum der Stadt Wien, Vienna, Austria.

Page 11. Painting of Franz Schubert on his way to school with his father. Johann Larwin (1873–1938).

Page 12. Autographed pen and ink on paper score for Franz Schubert's lieder "Trost." Text by Johann Mayrhofer, 1819.

Page 12. Inset. Oil on canvas portrait of Franz Schubert at age 17. Austrian School of painting. Kunsthistorisches Museum, Vienna, Austria.

Page 15. Portrait of Therese Grob (1800s). Anonymous. Historisches Museum der Stadt Wien, Vienna, Austria.

Page 15. Inset. Manuscript of Mass in F (1814) and the organ Schubert played at Liechtenthal Church. Vienna, Austria.

Page 16. *A Schubert Evening in a Vienna Salon.* Julius Schmid (1854–1935). Historisches Museum der Stadt Wien, Vienna, Austria.

Page 16. Inset. Portrait of Franz von Schober (1822). Leopold Kupelwieser (1796–1862). Historisches Museum der Stadt Wien, Vienna, Austria.

Page 19. Inset. Painting of the "Schubertianer," a circle of Schubert's friends (1820). Watercolor. Leopold Kupelwieser (1796–1862). Historisches Museum der Stadt Wien, Vienna, Austria.

Page 20. Inset. Portrait of Franz Schubert in mid-career. Leopold Kupelwieser (1796–1862). Gesellschaft der Musikfreunde, Vienna, Austria.

Page 22–23. Zseliz manor (1818). Gesellschaft der Musikfreunde, Vienna, Austria.

Page 23. Inset. *Schubert at the Piano* (1899). Oil on canvas. Gustav Klimt (1862–1918). Destroyed during WWII, this is a photograph of a reproduction.

Page 27. Schubert's reading glasses lie on top of "Die Taubenpost," the last of his lieder. Located in the apartment where Schubert died.

Web Sites

Due to the changing nature of Internet links, PowerKids Press has developed an online list of Web sites related to the subject of this book. This site is updated regularly. Please use this link to access the list: www.powerkidslinks.com/plfc/franz/